MW01231830

OSHA ROSE

Yoga for Relaxation

A guide to finding peace of mind through breathing exercises, restorative yoga postures, and meditation practices that can easily be incorporated into daily life.

First edition

This book was professionally typeset on Reedsy.
Find out more at reedsy.com

Contents

IV   Meditation

I

The Beginning

"We are what our thoughts have made us; so take care of what you think." —Swami Vivekananda

Acknowledgments

I am so grateful for the beautiful people who have blessed my daughter and I with love and support. Life is a journey of the soul. We rise, we fall, we fly, we are held, and we are all in this together. When we breathe deeply, we relax into the sweetness of each moment, deepen our connection with ourselves and with those whom we love the most. When we relax, it becomes easier to witness the synchronicities in life and to be thankful for it all.

Disclaimer

Always consult your healthcare provider and obtain medical clearance before practicing yoga postures or any other exercise program. It is recommended that yoga be practiced under the direct supervision of a qualified instructor. Practicing under the direct supervision and guidance of a qualified instructor may reduce the risk of injuries.

All yoga poses are not suitable for all persons. Practicing under the direct supervision of a qualified instructor and the direction of your healthcare provider can also help determine which poses are suitable for you. The information provided in this book is strictly for reference and is not in any manner a substitute for medical advice or the direct guidance of a yoga instructor.

The author, editors, publishers and distributors assume no responsibility or liability for any injuries or losses that may result from practicing yoga or any other breathing or exercise program in this book. The author, editors, publishers and distributors all make no representations or warranties with regards to the completeness or accuracy of information in this book, any linked websites, or other products represented herein.

Welcome

"Nothing in the universe can stop you from letting go and starting over." -Guy Finley

W elcome! If you are reading this book then a light in you was sparked. You aim to *take it easy* and *just*

relax. You are here to put in the effort and attain the peace of mind you desire in your life. I am honored to be the first to say *congratulations,* you are making your well-being a priority. The best news is you will continue getting better and better at calming the mind and relaxing into your life in the days to come. Relaxation is just a few deep breaths away. So breathe in, breathe out, and let's get started on the journey together now!

Introduction

"As long as you are breathing there is more right with you than wrong with you, no matter what is wrong."
-Jon Kabat Zinn

S o, you are reading this book. Have you stopped to consider why? What piqued your interest most about a book on yoga and relaxation? Is it a desire for a healthier lifestyle? Have you always been curious about yoga, just not interested in learning how to stand on your head? Is the stress in your life affecting your overall well-being and causing you to look for a holistic approach to your health? Is there a part of you that knows the peace you seek is already in you and hopes this book will wake up what lies dormant inside?

My name is *Osha Rose* and I have been a certified yoga teacher since 2008. In my years of teaching, I have led hundreds of students of all ages, shapes, and levels through yoga routines to help build strength and bring an awareness to the body. In the beginning, most public classes I taught were based on a fast-paced variation of hatha yoga called *vinyasa*.

Although I enjoy moving swiftly and connecting each inhale and exhale breath with a new pose, I have found the faster-paced classes can cause anxiety, frustration, and potentially create injuries for students who do not practice the yoga postures on a regular basis. While studying the biomechanics in the bodies of my yoga students, I noticed that the use of stabilizers like the wall, floor, or yoga blocks allows the body to relax more deeply into a yoga pose. When the body is supported, muscles stop contracting. While stabilized by the wall or the floor, the body develops an intelligence, an imprint, for safe alignment of its joints and limbs.

This book will help demystify the Sanskrit language, simplify the art of meditation, and guide you in a step-by-step fashion how to breathe and practice restoration based yoga poses. You will learn how to detach from the external stimuli periodically in your day by bringing your attention inward and concentrating on the movement of your breath.

The aim of this book and the direction in which I will guide you is towards relaxation of body and mind. I call the style of yoga in the following pages, *Yoga for Relaxation*. This book will cover three easy breathing techniques to integrate into your daily life. These practices will connect you to the relaxation response in your body by calming down your nervous system.

These breathing exercises, combined with the following easy-to-learn restorative poses, will help you tap into your body's innate wisdom and ability to heal.

I also share a guided meditation to connect you back to the wisdom rooted deep within.

I sincerely hope you enjoy!
    Osha

How to Use this Book

"When bringing attention to your breath, you are also setting an intention to slow down and be present."
-Osha Rose

T his book is designed to offer enjoyable, easy-to-follow breathing techniques and yoga postures with all the steps to guide you through the exercises from the comfort of your home. It is short, so reading it in its entirety before starting the yoga exercises is highly recommended. However, I do encourage you to follow along with the breathing exercises as you go. Actually, let's do a basic breathing exercise now to help you relax in preparation for what is ahead.

Basic Deep Breathing Exercise

- Gently breathe in through your nose.
- Slowly breathe out of your mouth releasing with an audible sigh, "Ahhhhh!"
- Again, breathe in through your nose.
- Slowly, gently, breathe out through your mouth extending your exhale slightly longer than your inhale.
- Inhale through the nose slowly taking in a little more breath into the lungs.
- Pause on full at the top of the breath and exhale gently through the mouth.

By bringing attention to your breath, you are also setting an intention to slow down and be present. With a little effort, dedication, and diligence you will discover that relaxation is only a breath or two away.

My hope is that while reading and following along with this book, you will experience the transformational effect of a yoga practice aimed at relaxation. It is a concise introduction to yoga and I hope it ignites your curiosity to learn more.

II

Yoga Postures

"Yoga is not about touching your toes. It is what you learn on the way down."
−Jigar Gor

What is Yoga and Do I need to learn Sanskrit?

"Sanskrit is such a sacred language that every syllable in every word has a vibration that is powerful and will affect you on a subtle level." –Osha Rose

Y oga originated in India over 5,000 years ago and is both a philosophical and spiritual practice. The word *Yoga* is derived from the Sanskrit root *Yuj* and it means to yoke,

17

unite or join together. Sanskrit is an ancient Hindu script, rich in entomology, where each word has deep meaning and is rooted in sacred sound. In order to practice yoga, it is not mandatory to learn Sanskrit, but you may enjoy giving it a try.

Sanskrit is such a sacred language that every syllable in every word has a vibration that is powerful and will affect you on a subtle level. So just for fun, as you read the Sanskrit words in this book, practice speaking these sacred sounds out loud. One word to say right now is Namaste. Pronounced Nah-ma-stay, when speaking this word we are saying, "The light in me sees and honors the light in you and together, we are one." Or more simply, "I bow to the light in you." Saying Namaste and physically bowing the head to hands in prayer position on the chest is how I like to close each yoga class that I teach.

The greeting of Namaste is a way to acknowledge our commonality as spiritual beings. In other eastern Asian cultures like Korea and Japan, the act of bowing is a common form of greeting and symbolic of reverence, a deep respect for the other. In America, we tend to shake hands upon initial meeting. It may feel more intimate than a slight bow, almost more so than a hug, since we have many nerve endings and active energetic pathways in our hands. This is why bringing hands together at the heart center is a healing gesture. We are energizing the multiple energy channels in our palms.

In the western part of the world, when we hear *yoga* many of us think about the physical movements in our body, such as touching our toes or lifting our leg over our head. The reality is, stretching and strengthening the body is only one of the eight steps that fully encompass the practices of yoga. According to the Hindu sage, Patanjali and his sacred text the *Yoga Sutras*, we must learn and practice the eight steps of the Ashtanga yoga system in order to cultivate balance and harmony of body, mind, and spirit. Patanjali describes the Ashtanga system as an eight limb path leading the yogi from the outer to the inner realms. The eight limbs in Sanskrit are: yama, niyama, asana, pranayama, pratyahara, dharana, dhyana and samadhi and are further explained below.

Yama – The word *yama* simply translates to *control* in English. The yamas teach moral restraint and the ethical duty to be mindful of our actions, thoughts and words. The five according to Patanjali's Yoga Sutras are: *Ahimsa* or non-violence, *Satya* or truthfulness, *Asteya* or non-stealing, *Brahmacharya* or self-restraint, and *Aparigraha* or non-coveting.

Niyama – These are considered virtuous habits and observances to couple with the yamas in order to engage in healthy living. They are: *Asana* or posture, *Pranayama* or breathing, *Pratyahara* or withdrawal of the senses, *Dharana* or concentration, *Dhyana* or meditation, and *Samadhi* or absorption.

Asana – This Sanskrit word literally means seat, posture, or place. Most yoga poses include *asana* at the end of the Sanskrit name because it is a posture or shape to take in your body, such as *Tadasana* for mountain pose.

Pranayama – An extension of life force energy through controlled breath, pranayama is a combination of the words, *prana* or life force energy and *ayama* to extend. Think of prana as the energy you first breathe in as a newborn and last exhale out as you leave your physical form. When you set an intention to extend your breath, you will bring in more life force energy and prolong your overall lifespan.

Pratyahara – To withdraw the senses is an important stage in yoga. This word is derived from the two roots in Sanskrit *prati*, which means to withdraw and *ahara,* which means food. In this fifth limb of yoga, it is not referring to a withdrawal from actual food, but from any external stimuli consumed with the mind. This limb is the foundation of meditation.

Dharana – Concentration is the definition of this sixth limb, a practice of steady focus of the mind on one thing so it becomes an effortless act. Use of a hand gesture or *mudra*, chanting a few Sanskrit words repeatedly as a mantra, or listening to the sounds of the breath are all ways to develop concentration.

Dhyana – When the seventh step is reached we experience a sense of calm, which is translated as contemplation or meditation. This step is the culmination of the preceding limbs and leads to the ultimate aim of yoga, which is enlightenment.

Samadhi – Translated as enlightenment or bliss, this final step of the Ashtanga yoga system is achieved only after we adjust our habits and behaviors, our physical bodies are exercised, our breathing is deepened, and we learn how to turn our gaze inward to study and fully be engrossed with the Self.

Can you remember the last time you felt *blissed-out*? A moment when you felt like you were in your element and completely satisfied in your life? If not, come back to this question later and trust that a memory will surface as you read on. If you *can* remember a time when you were fully absorbed in the moment, this is what bliss feels like.

Beginning with these eight limbs, my intention is to introduce to you a path that was outlined thousands of years ago to help you find contentment in your life. I invite you to dig a little deeper into the yamas and niyamas and take note of whether or not you are in alignment with these principles.

Start asking yourself, *am I kind in my thoughts, speech and actions?* You may find you are kinder to others than yourself or vice versa. Notice if you covet, hoard or steal, and how often you indulge in the things that bring you away from balance in your life. When we practice yoga with these eight limbs in mind, we move from a focus on *doing* to an awareness of our *being*.

You will be moving your body and breathing with the intention to relax in the pages that follow. The history of yoga and Sanskrit words are to help broaden your understanding of the word *yoga* and give it a more personal meaning for you.

The Benefits of Yoga

"Embodying the practices of yoga in a holistic way, being mindful of your speech and actions, will bring you closer to the people you love." -Osha Rose

Y ou chose this book because you already knew yoga can help you relax, but did you also realize that you can reduce blood pressure, aches and pains, and strengthen the endurance of your immune system just by taking a few deep breaths?

Yoga aids flexibility of mind and body, brightens overall mood, and can help you reach deeper levels of sleep when utilized routinely.

Yoga will even make it easier for you to cope with stress.

Embodying the practices of yoga in a holistic way, being mindful of your speech and actions, will also bring you closer to the people you love.

What is Restorative Yoga?

"Calming allows us to rest, and resting is a precondition for healing." –Thich Nhat Hanh

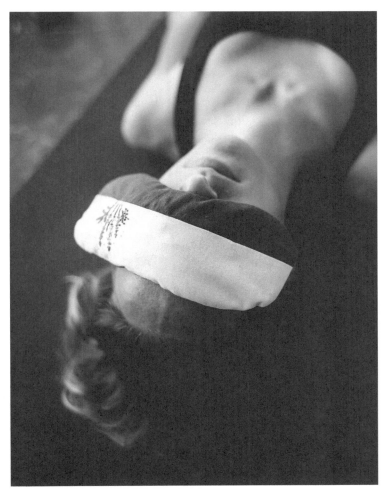

W hen you can surrender to gravity in a yoga pose and it feels like you could stay in that position for a few minutes with ease, it is likely a posture that will be restorative for your body. To increase support and encourage muscles to relax, restorative postures tend to be on the floor or against a wall. Props such as yoga blocks, straps, bolsters, blankets and eye pillows are also added to restorative positions to increase comfort, and to open and align parts of the body in a passive way.

In a typical hatha yoga class, students will be led through a series of poses called Sun Salutations or in Sanskrit, *Surya Namaskar*. The purpose of these movements is to wake up the physical body and to clear away any stagnant energy. The translation is to *worship that which gives us light.* The sun salutation variations move with a *vinyasa* flow, taking students from one posture to the next with a single inhale or exhale of breath. These classes are highly effective at building stamina in the body, and the repetition of poses brings focus from the mind into the body.

However, if you are unfamiliar with the sequence of poses or you like to take slower transitions between each posture, a vinyasa flow may bring on feelings of anxiousness. When I am a student in a vinyasa class, I too find it challenging to allow myself to fall behind the flow of class and honor my own internal pace. There is a natural inclination to keep up with the group and it may even *feel* better when everyone is moving in a synchronized way. As we practice, it is important to honor our unique body and its inherent rhythm.

Practicing restorative yoga poses is a great way to learn how to synchronize the body and the breath as you move. With longer holds in each posture, you have the time and space to explore the depths of your breathing and to develop a gentle rhythm in the body with the movement created by the act of breathing deeply. Transitions happen slowly with care and ease. What I love most about restorative yoga postures is that they tap into our innate healing systems.

Supported restorative poses will help relieve tension in the body, increase blood flow, and stimulate digestion. They also tend to bring on a sense of relaxation in the body almost immediately. Many yoga classes incorporate restorative postures into the end of class, such as Savasana when students lie on their backs in meditation.

Three Easy Restorative Poses

The following three postures provide a healthy foundation in your body to carry into your breathing and meditation practices so you feel properly aligned in your body when seated, standing or lying down.

Although you may be familiar with the poses, I invite you to receive these cues with fresh eyes and ears so you can be present in your body and give yourself what you need to feel supported.

We will use the wall, the floor, cushions, blankets and yoga blocks, if you have them, as props to modify each pose. The goal is for you to feel like you are resting in each position. Experiment with the props to determine which will best align the bones in your unique body.

Use the images to guide you.

Move slowly so you can listen to what your body needs in each moment. You will know that you are properly bolstered in the pose once it feels effortless to breathe there.

As you adjust yourself in each pose, back out if you feel any tension. Even if you have practiced these poses in the past, today is a brand new day for your body.

You may find that your hamstrings require extra support to alleviate tension in the low back this time around, or that your knees require support to ease tension in the inner thigh or groin area.

Listen to your body and respond with care.

Happy Easy Pose

Sukhasana

S ukhasana is derived from the Sanskrit word *sukham* which means joyful, easy, and comfortable. This cross-legged posture can help to improve your body's overall flexibility and promotes better integration of emotions and feelings in your brain.

Although this is *technically* an easy pose compared to say, a headstand, it may not be so easily attained in every *body.* If you know this is not a healthy position for you today, sit in a chair instead. In your chair slide your hips against the back of the seat, rest your hands in your lap, and firmly press your feet onto the floor.

Props to consider using for this pose:

Wall

Cushion

Yoga blocks

Firm blankets or large towels

(folded flat)

Experiment with sitting on a firm cushion or yoga block. The prop under your bottom should lift your torso so your hip crease is higher than your knees. Depending on how open your hips feel today, a firm blanket or large towel folded into a square may be all the lift you need. You may also like pillows or yoga blocks under your knees to relieve any tension in the groin area. Adding a folded blanket under your feet is another option for ankle support.

Place your cushion on the floor, against the wall, with the other props you will be using. You will know that you have found the props to use in this pose when you feel comfortable and at ease.

- **Gently lower your body** down to the floor. Sit on your prop with your ankles crossed and your back against the wall. You may want to add a folded blanket under your feet as a cushion for your feet.
- **Support your knees** with yoga blocks or pillows high enough to relieve any tension around the inner thighs.
- **Rest your palms on your knees** and bring your gaze downward. Feel the weight of your hips release into the support of the cushion beneath you.
- **Lift up out of your hips** to create space along your spine.
- **Gently press shoulder blades** towards the wall as you lift up through the chest. Feel the top of your head elevate towards the ceiling.
- **Imagine** there is a thin chord of string along your spine that extends out the crown of your head, reaching up towards the sky. Maintain this sensation of lift through the upper body and allow your back to feel stabilized by the wall.
- **Relax your shoulders** down away from your ears, resting shoulder blades on your back.
- **Open and close your jaw** and let your tongue rest on the roof of your mouth.
- **Try another position with your hands**, the *Dhyani Meditation mudra*. It may help you feel centered and more peaceful as you sit and breathe in this posture.
- **Place your right hand** in your lap with your palm facing up. Place your left hand on top of your right. Bring your thumbs to touch above your palms.
- **Keep your gaze** soft on the floor or to close your eyes completely.

Make any final adjustments, including opting to move to a firm chair if your body so requests. Take a few slow deep in-breaths through your nose breathing out through your mouth.

This is your supportive, happy, easy seated posture.

Next steps: Sit in this posture for your seated meditation and while you practice the alternate nostril breathing technique.

Mountain Pose

Tadasana

T adasana or mountain pose is the embodiment of *powerful stillness.* A basic standing posture, it is the foundational position for many standing yoga poses. Finding stillness in an upright position is empowering and elicits a deep sense of stability and strength from within. We will modify this pose and make it even more restorative for the body by resting the forehead on the wall, so a smooth wall is the only prop for this pose.

- **Stand facing a wall** with your hands resting by your sides.
- **Step forward** so your toes are nearly touching the wall.
- **Separate your feet** so you feel stable.
- **Move big toes** so they lightly brush against the wall.
- **Press down through your feet** to lift up through your chest.
- **Imagine** a chord along your spine lifting up and lengthening your entire torso through the top of your head.
- **Feel as if the crown of your head** is reaching up towards the sky.
- **Allow your gaze** to soften towards the floor and rest your forehead on the wall.
- **Keep your hands** resting by your sides or turn your wrists and rest your palms on the wall with your finger tips pointing down.
- **Relax your feet**, your face, and relax your neck and shoulders.
- **Close your eyes** and breathe deeply here for 10 breaths.

This is your properly aligned standing posture.

Next steps: Practice maintaining this posture in your body as you walk to your car or into a store. Do this pose a few times to imprint the alignment in your body before performing the walking meditation.

Corpse Pose

Savasana

S avasana in Sanskrit translates to *corpse* or *final resting pose.* A supine variation to the previous standing posture, this is an active resting pose that can be extremely healing for the body. When you lie on the floor you allow your vertebral column to realign and reset without any effort. The weight of your body releases into the downward energy of gravity, the fibers of facial tissue that connect bone to muscle loosen, and the thirty-one nerve pairs along your spine relax. Before assuming this supine posture, consider how you are feeling in your body to determine how best to proceed.

Props to consider using for this pose:
Mat or padded floor
Eye pillow or hand towel
Bolster or a Couch cushion
Firm blankets or large beach towels
(folded flat)

An eye pillow or small hand towel for your eyes is a helpful tool to encourage relaxation in the body. You can either close your eyes or find a non-moving object on the ceiling to focus upon if you choose not to use an eye cover.

Be sure to prop your knees with a bolster or a wide cushion. This lift and support connects your low back with the floor and takes tension out of your hamstrings along the back of your legs. If your head does not reach the floor, add a folded firm blanket or large towel under your head to connect your back body flush with the floor. This should align your chin level to the floor.

Once you have determined the props you will use, lay your yoga mat on the floor. Place the bolster next to it and be sure to grab something soft to drape over your eyes.

- **Gently lower your body** onto the floor and lie on your back with your knees bent, feet flat on the floor.
- **Slide your bolster or cushion** under your knees. If your

lower back was more comfortable with feet on the floor, return to that position, allowing your knees to gently rest together.

· **Relax the weight of your legs** onto the support of the cushion.

· **Place your eye pillow** over your eyes and rest both arms on the floor by your side, palms facing up.

· **Let your heels** grow heavy on the floor and slightly splay your feet out to either side.

· **Take a deep breath** in through your nose and sigh it out your mouth. Take a few more deep breaths just like that.

· **Allow your legs and arms** to grow heavy. Feel the weight of your entire body supported by the floor.

· **Scan your body** with your mind, feet, legs, hips, back, arms, neck, shoulders, face, and jaw.

· **Relax each area** that is still holding on and surrender into the feeling of being held by the floor and earth beneath you.

This is your safe and supported supine position.

Next steps: Return to this posture for the guided meditation at the end of this book and any time during the day when your body is asking you to rest.

III

Breathing

"Breathe. Let go. And remind yourself that this very moment is the only one you know you have for sure."
–Oprah Winfrey

The Relaxation Response

"If we listen to our body whisper, we will never have to hear it scream." –Bo Forbes

You have reached a state of relaxation when the body and mind are free of tension and anxiety. We learn from watching animals that shaking, sleeping, and stretching muscles are all effective ways to alleviate stress and cultivate this state of relaxation in the body. But have you ever wondered what is actually going on inside the brain when the body and mind relax? Before picking up this book, were you aware that your body is wired for relaxation if given the cue to do so?

Taking a deep breath gives your nervous system the signal that it is safe to relax. In response to upsetting news about your job, a loved one, or outside in the world around you, the brain activates the stress response with hormones like adrenaline and cortisol. When stressed, we tend to shallow-breathe or pant, taking in little to no new oxygen. It is deep breathing that informs the brain to produce mood-boosting endorphins. The simple act of breathing can help you remain calm under pressure and handle a stressful situation with more care and ease.

On a more scientific level, deep breaths inform your brain it is safe to switch over to the relaxation response, the parasympa-thetic nervous system. The parasympathetic nervous system is the part of the autonomic nervous system (or the ANS) that activates the body's ability to heal. This is essentially when the body deactivates the hyperarousal sequence or what is called the sympathetic fight-or-flight function of the nervous system.

The ANS is the part of the central nervous system that regulates involuntary body functions like breathing and digestion, and it is responsible for maintaining a state of homeostasis.

If you imagine the body is a computer, the nervous system is like the motherboard, the body's central command center. It originates from the brain and controls thinking, breathing, digestion, movement, and instinctive, automatic responses. Based on the brain's perception of the outer and inner stimuli, the motherboard knows when to switch between the sympa-thetic and parasympathetic nervous system automatically.

When a threat is detected, the hyperarousal sequence is activated. The body responds depending on the perceived stimuli, either by fighting, fleeing, freezing, or fawning. The brain is programmed to shut down all nonessential bodily functions so it can think and move more efficiently to get away from danger.

But when the brain signals the sympathetic nervous system, it releases stress hormones that shut down the rest and digest functions like the immune and digestive systems. The body stops producing the happy chemicals that serve as natural pain relievers to focus all of its energy on survival. This activation of the sympathetic nervous system is meant to be temporary. In order to maintain balance and overall health, the relaxation response must be turned back on once the danger is evaded.

Although more complex than other mammals' brains, the human nervous system has not evolved much over the past few thousand years. The influx of technology, especially in the past 20 years with the smartphone, has caused our primitive nervous system to remain stuck in fight-or-flight mode due to an overwhelming increase in the demands of our workloads and personal relationships. Our reception of email and text messages, voicemails, news articles and social media alerts all cause fear, panic, and ultimately a shutdown of our vital bodily functions.

This natural response is part of the body's intricate system designed to focus energy on the stressors at hand, and ultimately protect us from harm. We likely do not have to fear being chased in a forest as prey, yet our brains will automatically activate the sympathetic nervous system when we see the blue lights of a police car in the rear view mirror of our car, or when we think about a future event with feelings of fear and anxiety. Our brains react as if it were a life or death situation, just as it did 300,000 years ago when we were primates on the hunt.

Many of us live with the sympathetic side of the nervous system chronically activated. This causes exhausted adrenal glands, an inability to process and digest foods, and ultimately *dis*-ease in our bodies. It is important to remember the body seeks balance.

To heal and repair like other animals do, we must honor our body's primal instinct to breathe, sleep, and rest in order to turn back on the parasympathetic nervous system. Your breath is almost an instant way to reach equilibrium. Remembering to take a breath before reacting to stressors will help regulate your autonomic nervous system.

So if all we have to do is breathe deep, then why are the nervous systems of so many chronically stuck in the mode of fight-or-flight? Because timing is everything. When the time is right, a book like this one will cross the path of whomever is ready for change.

For those living in pain, fear, or with anxiety, it may take a major life event to lead them to the path of health. Once there is a strong enough desire to create a positive shift, the dedication of time and energy to a new routine usually follows. It is then that we can adopt the practice of listening to our body whisper before something more grave occurs to make it scream.

Trust that now is the perfect time for you to be learning about your nervous system and the subtle changes you can make to your habits to bring harmony into your mind and body. You are exactly where you are meant to be at precisely the right time.

Three Easy Breathing Techniques

"When you own your breath, nobody can steal your peace."
-Unknown

The following breathing techniques will turn on the relaxation response in your nervous system and tap into your body's innate ability to heal. They have been modified to increase ease of use, lessen feelings of anxiousness, and to reduce mental resistance.

Pick a technique to practice for 5 minutes a day for the next two days.

Try all three exercises a few times and choose one to practice every day. Start with a five minute timer and be sure to select a calming sound like a bell or chime. After a few days, start increasing the duration by 1 minute each day, so that in two weeks you will be deep breathing for 15 minutes a day. Notice how you feel before you start compared to how you feel afterwards.

You will find that breathing deeply, even for just one minute, increases your emotional intelligence and will bring you into a deeper state of awareness of your body, mind and spirit.

The purpose of each exercise is to guide your brain to the relaxation response in the body.

If for any reason a technique feels stressful or causes anxiety in your body, move to the next one or return to the basic deep breathing technique of inhaling through the nose and exhaling through the mouth, extending the exhale slightly longer than each inhale.

Box Breathing

Sama Vritti Pranayama

T he box breathing technique, also referred to as square breathing, is a gentle way to calm the mind and introduce a sensation of connection between the mind and body. This form of breathing was named Sama Vritti Pranayama in Sanskrit for its *equal parts of flow*. Used by the US Navy Seals to aid in stress management, this easy yet powerful technique divides your breathing into four steps.

A great time of day to practice this exercise is in the evening before bed. You can choose to lie in bed and practice instead of seated as well. Box breathing will have a similar effect on the mind like counting sheep, distracting you from mental chatter. It also encourages your body to relax into the mode of rest and digest to expedite falling asleep.

The basic concept is to visualize drawing the four sides of a square with a four-count breath. You will inhale up one side, hold your breath in across the top, exhale down the other side, and hold out the breath as you imagine the bottom line of the square.

We will use an even, four-beat count on each of the four sides. It will match the time it takes you to say, *one Mississippi, two Mississippi, three Mississippi, four Mississippi.* The inhale is through your nose and the exhale is out of your mouth.

To increase the positive effects on the brain, visualize the inhale bringing in clear, white, calming energy. As you exhale, feel a physical release of any tension in the neck, shoulders, and any other areas where you feel tense.

- **Find a comfortable seat on a chair** with your feet evenly connected to the floor.
- **Set a 5 minute timer** with a calming sound.
- **Bring your attention** to your body. Notice that you are automatically breathing in and assimilating fresh, clean oxygen and exhaling carbon dioxide.

Without making any changes yet, notice if there is depth to your inhale or length to your exhale. Are you breathing through your nose or your mouth?

- **Bring in a deeper breath** through the nostrils, and slowly exhale out your mouth.
- **Slow down your inhale** even more, and gently extend your exhale.
- **Inhale deep into your belly**, allowing your lungs to fill up your chest.
- **Hold this breath in** for a moment, then let it out until you feel your lungs completely empty.
- **Hold the breath out**. As you pause here, notice how it feels to be empty of all breath.
- **Draw in another slow, long inhale** through your nose. Feel your lungs fill up with cleansing, clean oxygen.
- **Pause to acknowledge the sensation** of fullness, and then slowly send the breath back out the mouth.
- **Pause here on empty** and prepare to lengthen the next inhale to a count of *four Mississippi's*, imagining the breath traveling up the right side of a square.
- **Inhaling count silently:** one Mississippi, two Mississippi, three Mississippi, four Mississippi.
- **Hold the breath in for the same length and count**, while imagining the breath resting on the top line of the square.
- **Exhale through the mouth** to the count of *four Mississippi's*. See the breath in your mind traveling down the left side of the square.
- **Hold with a pause on empty** and count to four. Resting at the bottom of the square.
- **Keep going at a pace that feels best** for you, matching the

length of breath and pause as you count to four on each side of the square in your mind.

· **Focus on the sensation** of fullness at the top of the square, when you breathe in and hold.
· **Exhale** and imagine the breath sliding down the left side of the box and return to the bottom.

Experience the sensation of empty before bringing breath back in through the nose. These pauses in between breaths are when we are calming down our internal nervous system. The deliberate breathing is signaling the brain to turn off our sympathetic nervous system and to turn on the parasympathetic *rest and digest* function.

This will inform the body to stop producing cortisol and move out of fight-or-flight mode, which enables other vital systems like our body's immune and digestive systems to turn back on. Your slower breathing calms the heart and blood pressure, which helps you think more clearly.

Our bodies do not know the difference between external stressors in your environment versus the internal stress caused by thinking about stressors. Since all types of stress activate your sympathetic nervous system, each should be countered with a relaxation practice as soon as you notice the fight-or-flight sequence has been activated, or once you are physically out of harm's way.

Taking just one deep breath will help to reconnect with relaxation in your nervous system. This is important especially when experiencing feelings of anxiousness or overwhelm, since in those moments you are likely panting or barely breathing at all.

Next steps: Once your timer sounds, take a few easy breaths and notice how you feel. Take a moment to write down these feelings.

Alternate Nostril Breathing

Nadi Shodhana Pranayama

I n Sanskrit, Nadi Shodhana Pranayama means *purification of the channel.* An excellent technique to help alleviate anxiety, this breathing exercise is a cleaning-of-the-slate that will have a subtle, yet profound effect on your nervous system. The ideal time to practice this breathing technique is first thing in the morning with a straight spine in a comfortable seated position.

The nickname of this breathing exercise is alternating nostril breathing because in its full expression it involves inhaling and exhaling through one nostril at a time. However, in this variation that follows we will only practice breathing in and out of the left nostril to keep it simple. Practice this technique for 2 to 3 minutes.

- **Start by finding a seated position** that you can comfortably hold for a few minutes with your back straight, either on the floor or in a chair.
- **Set a 2 minute timer** with a calming sound like a bell or chime.
- **Take a few gentle breaths** in through your nose and out through your mouth.
- **Notice if you need to blow clear** the pathway to your nose and take a deep breath in and a long slow breathe out.
- **Feel a release** around your neck and shoulders with each exhale.
- **Imagine** you are putting down any weight or burden you have been carrying on your back.
- **Breathe in through the nose** and exhale out your mouth, bringing your gaze towards the floor.
- **Allow your eyes to close**, if that feels good in your body. Bring your gaze from behind your eyelids, up towards your pineal gland between your eyebrows.
- **Use your right thumb** to block off your right nostril and extend your other fingers towards the sky. If holding fingers upright becomes uncomfortable, let them rest on your forehead.

- **Inhale slowly** through the left nostril, pause, and slowly exhale through the same side.
- **Take another deep breath in** through the left nostril, pause to hold the breath in.
- **Exhale** through your left nostril and pause to hold the breath out.
- **Breathe in** through the left side of your nose. Pause for a moment on full.
- **Exhale** the breath back out the left nostril. Pause to hold the breath out.
- **Inhale** again through the left side of your nose and pause once you fill up your lungs.
- **Continue breathing slowly** in and out through the left nostril. Remember to slow down and pause between the inhale and exhale.

Practice breathing just like this until the timer goes off.

Take a few more breaths with both hands in your lap. Notice how you feel once the timer brings you back. You may feel calm, at peace, even bliss.

It could feel as if you wiped the slate of your mind clean and you are now experiencing pure feelings of pleasure trickling down from the brain. If so, this is the limbic system that experiences and expresses pleasure emotions and tells the body it is happy.

Next steps: When you rise each day, instead of checking the alerts or notifications on your phone, set a five minute timer to breathe.

Everything and everyone, including you, will benefit from your choice to breathe first, before introducing your brain to the outer stimulus of your day.

Ocean Breath

Ujjayi Pranayama

R eferred to as ocean breath, Ujjayi Pranayama is a form of breath control that sounds like the waves of the ocean or a quiet snore. Translated as *victorious breath*, this exercise is highly effective in aligning with the flow of your energetic channel along the spinal column. If you are familiar with the Star Wars movies, this breathing technique is also referred to as the Darth Vader breath for its unique tone, similar to the sound you make when you breathe on a mirror to fog it up.

To begin, start with the basic deep breathing exercise and come to a comfortable seat. If you are uncomfortable sitting upright today, practice ocean breathing lying on the floor, a bed, or on a couch.

- **Set a 5 minute timer** with a gentle sound for your alarm.
- **Allow your gaze to soften** and shift downward towards the floor. Eventually shut your eyes completely, if that feels easy to do.
- **Feel the opposing energy** of your spine lengthening up out of your seat and the weight of your hips sinking down into your chair.
- **Let your shoulder blades** settle downwards onto your back. If lying on your back, you will surrender completely into the support beneath your body.
- **Now inhale** through the nose, lift your right hand in front of your mouth, and pretend you are fogging up an imaginary mirror in your hand as you exhale out your mouth into your palm.
- **Close your mouth** and maintain this slight constriction in the throat on your inhale, being mindful the air touches the throat and not the inside of the nose.
- **Exhale** emitting the ocean-like sound with the mouth closed as your throat gently contracts, resting both hands in your lap.
- **Keep breathing** and slowly increase the decibel level with each exhale.

- **You will begin to release a *hiss* sound** as the air touches your throat and you relax into the wave of sound this breathing generates in your body.
- **Imagine** you are a surfer riding the waves of your emotions. See each in-breath bringing you up to the crest of each wave of joy, anxiety, pleasure, or frustration. With each out-breath, see yourself cruising through the tube of the wave, riding each emotion into shore with ease and grace.

Keep breathing here until you hear your timer chime. Return to an easy breath and take a moment to feel into your body and notice any sensations.

Next steps: As you progress in duration with this technique, challenge yourself to bring it out into your day. Remember your *Ujjayi-victorious-ocean-breath* as you wait for your turn at a traffic light, or as you stand in line at the grocery store. Focus on creating a hissing sound with both the inhale and exhale breath.

And if you share a bed with a Darth-Vader-wanna-be, their snoring can now serve as a cue to practice riding the waves of your emotions with this breathing technique while lying next to them in bed.

IV

Meditation

"You change the world by being yourself."
−Yoko Ono

What is Meditation and How do I know if it's working?

"Unease, anxiety, tension, stress, worry — all forms of fear — are caused by too much future, and not enough presence."
-Eckart Tolle

D o you have a preconceived notion about meditation? Do you think it is tied to a religion or that you must be a spiritual person to meditate? Could meditation be a mental shift that is so simple we can all do it with a little effort? But why meditate at all? What is the point of putting in the effort?

Meditation brings our bodies back to a natural state of equilibrium by alleviating anxiety, worry and stress. As Patanjali describes in his eight limbs of yoga, when we practice meditating we are developing our concentration, relaxing the hyperactivity of our minds, and remembering who we really are in this present moment.

Meditation in Tibet simply means *to become familiar with your mind.* It translates from Sanskrit *to cultivate an awareness.* Meditation practices vary widely, but what they all have in common is the aim of turning your attention inward. When you are first getting started, it is best to find a quiet place where you can sit comfortably with little distractions. The exercise of meditation is to practice focusing your mind on your breath, a hand gesture, or the sounds around you for a set duration of time.

In a yoga class, students lie on their backs for a brief meditation at the end of class. When you move energy with physical postures, like in a yoga class, it gets easier to settle into meditation. Lying down is also a good way to introduce stillness into the body, since most of us associate sleep with being in a horizontal position.

If you have experienced those five minutes lying quietly on the floor in a yoga class, it may have felt really challenging for you to be still or it may have felt incredible, like a vacation from your thoughts and worries. Some of my students have even fallen into a deep slumber in that short period of time. When you can reach that state of rest, it is as if nothing else matters.

If not in a yoga class, you may have experienced a meditative state of mind while relaxing in your favorite chair, watching the sky fill with color at sunset, or when you observed a child dancing to the beat of her own drum. A feeling similar to what Patanjali called the final step in the Ashtanga yoga system, Samadhi or bliss.

There are stages to the depths you can reach in meditation, and each time you practice you grow closer to that ultimate stage of bliss. Your progression is not measured by which level or limb attained, but in how you work through the resistance of the mind. What matters is your ability to breathe into the discomfort and sit with it.

The information in this book will plant a seed within you. It is an offering with options and a starting place. Your next step is then to take your practice off these pages and into your daily life. As you sample the breathing exercises and restorative yoga poses with your meditation practice, notice any changes in your physical and mental health to track your progress.

Pick a meditation and commit to a 5 to 15 minute practice for three weeks.

You will ride the wave of emotions as you breathe through the challenge of being still. After a few weeks of practice, you will see how meditation eases the mind and reduces the effects of stress on the body. Your newfound health will become your motivation to continue practicing and to discover deeper levels of meditation.

Meditation is a tool to help us become aware of our actions, so we have more compassion for ourselves and others, and to help us respond to challenges in our lives with grace. It may be a walking meditation where you notice how your feet touch the ground walking from your car to your office building, or a seated morning meditation where you listen to the sounds of your home and breathe on a cushion in your living room.

Your meditation might be listening along to a recording that guides you into a relaxing state or just those five marvelous minutes at the end of a yoga class. In the beginning, meditation for you may simply be for 30 seconds in the shower when you take a few deep breaths and momentarily disconnect from the chatter in your mind.

How do you know if meditation is really working?

You can track your progress to determine if meditation is working by measuring the electrical activity of the brain, called brain waves. These waves are formed when a burst of electrical pulses are sent from one group of neurons to another.

Waves are measured in speed cycles per second called hertz, and abbreviated as Hz. If you are awake and alert, the waves might be very fast, or if you are resting or sleeping, they might be very slow. The waveforms will change based on how you feel and what you are thinking or doing. Ranging from fastest to slowest, the main four brain wave levels are: Beta, Alpha, Theta, and Delta.

When we are actively going about our day, our brain is in the problem-solving Beta state. When we are in a deep sleep we are at the Delta level. Many of us are likely operating in a high level of Beta during the busy active hours of our day. It is when the brain waves slow down to Alpha or Theta that we will notice we are relaxed.

An electroencephalogram (an EEG) is one of the first ways discovered to observe human brain activity in a non-intrusive way. This method is still used to record brain waves through electrode sensors attached to the scalp. Once we become aware of our breathing, our respiratory system will also clue us in on our neurological activities without the need of such a machine.

When certain areas of the brain are overaroused, we are in the sympathetic fight-or-flight mode and the nervous system is on high alert. You may experience shortness of breath, increased heart rate, and other symptoms such as anxiety, aggression, nightmares or other sleep problems. This active mind creates higher levels of Beta brain wave forms close to 20 or even 30 Hz, sending energy bursts that look like tight, jagged lines through the brain.

Wherever you are right now, pause reading this book and take a few deep breaths.

Breathing in through the nose and sighing out through the mouth. Do this at least three times, letting each exhale be a little longer than the previous one.

If your brain waves were measured at this moment, after calming your nervous system by breathing, these oscillating electrical voltages are likely down near 8 Hz, closer to the Alpha relaxed reflection state. It is in this state when athletes perform their best. If you are somewhere lying down or sitting with your eyes closed, you may have also breathed long enough to reach Theta waveforms. In the Theta realm you are in a meditative state, where many experience creative downloads.

By withdrawing from outer stimulation, even just for these few moments like we just did, we enable our brain activity to slow down to a more restful level. We enable the metabolization, digestion, and immunity functions of our body to turn back on because our sympathetic nervous system takes this slower breathing as a cue to take a break.

Each breath gives the body the message of how safe and steady you feel, and also brings more oxygen to the thinking brain. When we move from overactive Beta brain waves at 12 to 35 Hz down to the reflective Alpha brain waves at 8 to 12 Hz, thoughts become less scattered, creativity is restored and our overall approach to the day can be revitalized.

If you are curious about measuring your brain waves to see how breathing affects you, buy a headset version of the EEG. And if you would like to get a sense of where you are at any given moment, notice your level of focus and engagement on a task. Taking a few breaths will usually slow the heartbeat and bring you out of the higher Beta range. Once you are in a more reflective state of Alpha or Theta your breathing will become slow and steady.

There is also Gamma, which is the fifth and highest level of brain waveforms but it is hard to measure with an EEG. The Gamma state is when the brain, like a car functioning optimally, is firing on all cylinders and operating with a heightened awareness. This is when one feels hyper-focused and able to process information in a highly efficient manner. The brain tends to produce Gamma waves when intensely focused or actively engaged. You may reach what feels like a Gamma-state after you attain extended periods in a seated meditation. You will know because you will feel clear, focused, and able to immerse yourself in a project that requires brainpower.

Many of us are functioning with an overly active Beta wave level oscillating near 35 Hz. When we live with our brains on overdrive, we are exhausting our adrenals. This overarousal of the sympathetic, fight-or-flight functions can also make it difficult to concentrate. To begin to counter these effects, it may be as simple as taking three deep breaths, sitting without distractions for a few minutes, or reading a book like this.

You are learning how to relax right here and now, and this will help to bring your nervous system and brain wave forms back into balance. When you can grow still in body and mind, you will experience the inner peace of meditation. The aim then becomes to maintain this deeper level of consciousness as you interact with your environment and others in your daily life.

Walking Meditation

An easy way to practice meditation is by walking in a mindful manner. This is a practice of becoming aware of your body as you physically move it through space. Practice barefoot in a private place where you can walk back and forth in a line unobserved. Each time you practice you will choose something to focus on for a set amount of time, such as your breath, legs or feet.

For this first walking meditation, you will focus on your feet to keep it simple.

To prepare, clear an area where you can take five steps before turning around and remove your shoes and socks.

- **Set a 5 minute timer** with a soothing sound.
- **Assume a relaxed standing position** with your body.
- **Gently adjust your arms** by your side or on your hips so they feel comfortable.
- **Bring your weight into your right foot** and slowly pick up the left.
- **Move your left foot** with all your awareness so that every slight motion is felt.
- **Feel your toes press down** as you lift your heel and prepare to take your first step.
- **Become aware of your left foot** moving through space and as you place it a few inches forward and step.
- **Feel your heel** as it connects back down with the floor, and notice how your toes follow the heel.
- **Connect your left foot** completely with the floor, shifting your weight into this side, and prepare to step with the right foot.
- **Move slowly** and with all your focus on your feet.
- **Feel your toes press down** as you lift your heel and prepare to take your next step.
- **Become aware of your right foot** and how it moves through space and again connects with the floor.
- **Slowly place your heel** and sense it as it touches the surface of your floor.
- **Feel the arch of your foot** as you roll through to your toes

and connect your right foot completely with the floor.

If you find it challenging to balance, try moving at a slightly faster pace, walking next to the wall, or sliding your toes along the floor instead of picking up your foot.

Gently breathe as you go, making every detail of your foot-in-motion the focal point of your practice.

- **Notice if your mind wanders** to your thoughts and bring it back to your feet.
- **Continue moving very slowly**, begin to notice each little minutiae of your step—the up, the down, the in between.
- **Notice what distracts you** and remember the aim is not to stop thinking.

Your practice is to observe the mind and bring it back to your focal point if it wanders from your feet, no matter how many times.

As you gently move across this small area, you may see your surroundings in a new light and your ability to sense and feel may also heighten.

Next step: When your timer sounds, take a few deep breaths and write down a word or two to describe how you feel.

Seated Meditation

S itting in meditation invites a balance of focus and relaxation into the body. For this exercise you will combine your knowledge of the happy easy seated pose and the box breathing technique to practice this seated meditation.

The aim of this exercise is for you to become familiar with the sounds around you in your environment. Although gentle music is helpful in bringing the mind into a relaxed state, practice in silence so you can learn to use your senses to connect with your surroundings on a deeper level.

When you practice in silence using a hand gesture can help you concentrate. The hand position we will practice here is called *Shunya Mudra* and means the Gesture of Emptiness. The shunya mudra is also a gesture of spaciousness and is thought to provide relief from a range of hearing and balance issues, such as vertigo and numbness in the body. Try it now by touching your middle finger to thumb on each hand.

Begin your meditation by first setting a timer for 5 minutes. Remember to select an alarm tone that is soothing.

- **Gently lower yourself down** to sit on a cushion or yoga block, with your ankles crossed and your back against a wall. If sitting on the floor is not available in your body today, sit on a chair with a firm back.
- **Add props** you that will help you feel supported, like a pillow under each knee, or a blanket under your ankles.
- **Rest your hands** on your knees with palms facing up and let your gaze soften towards the floor.
- **Keep the back of your hands** on your knees, bring your middle finger to touch your thumb for the gesture of emptiness with both hands.
- **Take a few slow, deep in-breaths** through the nose exhaling with a sigh out the mouth.
- **Relax your hips and legs** into the support of the floor beneath you.
- **Lift up out of your hips** to create space along your spine.
- **Gently press shoulder blades** towards the wall as you lift up through the chest. If you find there are props you would like to add or remove, do so now.
- **Feel the top of your head** elevate towards the ceiling.

- **Imagine there is a thin chord of string** along your spine that extends out the crown of your head, reaching up towards the sky.
- **Maintain this sensation of lift** through the upper body while you allow your back to be stabilized on the wall.
- **Relax your shoulders** down away from your ears, resting shoulder blades on your back.
- **Bring in a breath**, deep into your belly, allowing your lungs to fill up your chest.
- **Hold this breath in** for a moment, then let it out until you feel your lungs completely empty.
- **Hold the breath out** for a moment. As you pause here, notice how it feels to be empty of breath.
- **Draw in another long, slow inhale** through your nose. Feel your lungs fill up with fresh, clean air.
- **Pause to acknowledge the sensation** of fullness, and then slowly send the breath back out the mouth.
- **Bring the image of a square** to mind.
- **Pause on empty** and prepare to lengthen the next inhale to a count of four *Mississippi's*.
- **Inhaling count silently**, one Mississippi, two Mississippi, three Mississippi, four Mississippi, imagining the breath traveling up the right side of your square.
- **Hold the breath in** for the same count of four and imagine the breath resting on the top line of the square.
- **Exhale through the mouth** to the count of four.
- **See the breath traveling** down the left side of the square in your mind.
- **Hold with a pause on empty** and count to four, resting at the bottom of the square.

Keep breathing, slowly pausing after each inhale and exhale, letting the tempo be what feels good to you. Allow the breath to match in length as you count to four on each side of the square in your mind. Listen to your body and make any adjustments if you are no longer comfortable in your current position.

Allow yourself to shift back into a gentle deep breathing, no longer counting. Bring your awareness into the space around you.

Do you notice any sounds that may not have been in your periphery before now? Perhaps the humming of a fan or the sound of a car driving by outside your window? Can you notice what sounds your own body is making as you breathe?

Continue listening and breathing until your alarm sounds.

Next steps: When your time here concludes, take a few deep breaths to seal in the experience. Write a note to yourself to document how you now feel.

Guided Meditation

"Logic will get you from A to B. Imagination will take you everywhere." –Albert Einstein

A guided meditation is a form of meditation where you listen to the voice of a teacher as they lead you through the practice. It is a great place to start your journey into meditation since you will be instructed on what to do with your body, mind, and breath each step of the way.

Guided meditation may even become the easiest path to relaxation for you, once you find a guided meditation you really enjoy.

In the following exercise, you will lie on your back, close your eyes, and allow yourself to be led into a relaxed state through guided imagery.

You will go into the woods in your mind and experience the smells, sights, sounds, and textures of the earth and trees around you. All you will do is listen and breathe, and even the listening part may fade into the background at points along the way.

Please note: only the audio version of this book will include the recording read by the author.

Before we begin, take a moment to connect with your body to determine if lying on the floor on your back is the best way to proceed. It is important that you practice tuning into your body before each exercise. This will ensure you properly modify your movements to meet the needs of your body.

Close your eyes, put your hand on your heart, and take in a slow inhale breath. Exhale the breath and ask yourself, *how would I like to be positioned for the next 15 minutes* and listen to the answer.

If you prefer to be in a position other than lying on the floor now, move to lie on your couch, bed, or take a seat in a comfortable chair. As you are guided onto the floor, just imagine yourself taking the corpse pose and remain where you are.

- **Lay a yoga mat on the floor** or decide where you will lie that is padded.
- **Gather the other props** you would like to use, such as a bolster or cushion for under your knees, eye pillow or hand towel, maybe a folded blanket for under your head, and another blanket to spread over the top of you.
- **Place the props** near where you will lie down. If you are using a folded blanket under your head to level your chin, position the folded blanket where your head will rest.

You are ready to begin your 10 minute guided meditation.

- **Gently lower your body onto the floor** and lie on your back with your knees bent, feet flat on the floor.
- **Slide your bolster or cushion under your knees**. If you find it feels more comfortable for your lower back with bent knees, return to that position with knees knocked together.
- **Relax the weight of your legs** onto the cushion.
- **Place your eye pillow** or a small towel over your eyes.
- **Bring the blanket** over your body to cover yourself.
- **Rest both arms** on the floor by your side, palms facing up.
- **Place palms down** on your belly, while keeping elbows and upper arms on the floor.
- **Let your feet slightly splay** out to either side.
- **Take a deep breath** in through your nose and sigh it out your mouth.

- **Take a few more deep breaths**, letting your exhale be slightly longer than your inhale.
- **Allow your legs and arms to grow heavy**. Feel the weight of your entire body supported by the floor beneath you.
- **Relax any parts of your body that are still tense** or holding on in some way.
- **Feel the muscles in your jaw relax**.
- **Let the muscles and skin around your eyes** soften.
- **Rest your tongue gently** on the roof of your mouth and bring an awareness to the muscles in your neck and shoulders.
- **Feel your neck and shoulders relax** into the support of the floor beneath you.
- **Tune into the rhythm of your breathing**.
- **Feel the breath coming in** through your nose and notice if there is a temperature to the air as it moves into your body. Is it warm? Cool?
- **Close your mouth** on your next exhale and breathe out of your nose. If that feels good in your body, let the inhale and exhale continue to move in and out through your nose.
- **Allow the skin on your forehead** to relax and be smooth.
- **Allow your throat** to relax and feel the corners of your mouth lift into a gentle smile.

Now imagine you are in the woods in your favorite place to connect with the trees in nature.

Take a deep breath in and notice what you smell. Do you smell the trees? The earth? Are there any other scents in the air?

Imagine you are stretching your arms out wide to either side as you take another deep breath in and lift your chest towards the sky. Close your eyes and lift your face up towards the sun. Feel the warmth of its rays upon your skin.

Now look around you. What do you see? Are there ferns, mushrooms, or fallen leaves on the ground? Are there big tall trees in front of you? Small saplings just sprouting up? Can you see the thick gnarly roots of the tall trees? What is nearest to you? Can you reach out and touch anything?

Bring your gaze onto a nearby tree. Take note of which tree you see. Is it a small evergreen just taking root and the same height as you are? Or maybe you see a thin white birch tree? An old oak tree with thick hard layers of bark? Or a huge willow tree with long branches and leaves draping down over you, that you can look up and into from where you stand. Or perhaps you are in a tropical setting and it is a tall smooth king palm tree that you gaze upon.

Take in all the features of this tree. Notice its height compared to you and the other trees around it. What color is the bark? Does it have leaves? Green needles? Acorns or pine cones? Reach for the tree and touch it. Feel the temperature of its trunk. Is it warm from the sunshine? What does the texture feel like against your hand? Is it smooth and calming? Is it dry and peeling? Is it sticky with oozing sap?

Take a deep breath in and imagine what it might feel like to be the tree. What kind of life has it had so far? How does this tree stay alive? What gives it life? Its roots? The rain and sunshine?

Can you imagine all the seasons this tree has withstood? All the

84

weather? The animals and insects for which it has provided food and shelter? Imagine you are watching this tree as it ebbs and flows with the cycles of the earth. As it draws into itself all the nutrients it requires from above and below.

Now take a slow, deep breath connecting back into your body and imagine you are this tree. As you breathe, imagine you can feel the ground as it pulsates around your roots. Inhale through your nose and imagine your body is the trunk of the tree. Feel yourself receiving all the healing nutrients you need in this moment from the earth.

Breathe slowly in and out and imagine you are bringing the oxygen up through your roots into your center, your trunk, and it is filtered by the earth before it enters into your lungs. Each breath as it comes in, fills you up, relaxing your limbs. Imagine you can taste the sweetness of the soil.

As you exhale you clear anything blocking you from receiving the light from above. Imagine you can feel the warmth of the sun on your branches and leaves. Sense that your breath is enriching your roots and nourishing your soul as it smooths any frayed edges of your bark.

Fully embody the tree. *Be* the tree.

Allow the chatter in your mind to blow through your branches like the wind. Feel your roots anchoring you into the earth, source, your foundation. Sense that everything you need is already within you. Keep breathing here. Rooted in your power. You are stable, able, and strong.

Right here in your body, mind and spirit.

Now bring a few more slow, deep breaths in and out of your lungs. Imagine you are again standing next to this tree. Notice how you feel now, after being fully immersed in the spirit of the tree.

Take a moment to acknowledge the tree and its surroundings one more time.

Slowly start to bring your awareness back into your physical body. Gently wiggle your toes and fingers, easing yourself back into your space. Continue breathing at a natural pace, and feel into your body. Stretch your arms, legs, and open and close your jaw.

Think of a word or phrase to describe how you feel. Calm? Rested? Confident? A sense of inner wisdom?

Next step: When you are ready to rise, write this word or phrase down adding any other thoughts or feelings you experienced during this guided meditation.

Resources

"Knowledge is power. Information is liberating. Education is the premise of progress, in every society, in every family."
-Kofi Annan

Singhdeo, A. (2023, September 25). *History of Yoga: Origin & Evolution.* https://www.shvasa.com/yoga-blog/history-of-yoga#:~:text=Yoga%20originated%20in%20ancient%20India,promote%20spiritual%20growth%20and%20understanding

India, E. (2023, May 18). The importance of Sanskrit in understanding Hindu Scriptures. *Medium.* https://medium.com/@exoticindiaa/the-importance-of-sanskrit-in-understanding-hindu-scriptures-82f107d9621b

Sharma, M. (2021, July 7). *Practicing the 8 limbs of yoga will help you understand yoga as it was meant to be.* Healthline. https://www.healthline.com/health/fitness/the-8-limbs-of-yoga#:~:text=The%20journey%20of%20the%20eight,in%20the%20present%20moment%20indefinitely.

Burgin, T. (2021, March 29). The Five Yamas of Yoga: Definition

& Practice Tips · Yoga Basics. *Yoga Basics.* https://www.yogabas
ics.com/learn/the-five-yamas-of-yoga/

Pranayama in yoga. (n.d.). Yoga. https://www.keralatourism.or
g/yoga/popular-asanas/prana-asana#:~:text=The%20Sanskri
t%20word%20%E2%80%9Cprana%E2%80%9D%20refers,br
eathes%20pervades%20the%20entire%20being

MasterClass. (2021, June 7). *How to Practice Pratyahara: A Guide
to the Fifth Limb of Yoga.* Retrieved November 22, 2023, from
https://www.masterclass.com/articles/pratyahara-yoga-guide
#

Sater-Wee, D. (2023, March 2). *Hand pressure points: everything
you need to know.* American Institute of Alternative Medicine.
https://www.aiam.edu/acupuncture/hand-acupuncture-points
/

Burke, A. (2015, November 30). *A restorative practice inspired by
Vinyasa.* https://yogainternational.com/article/view/a-restorat
ive-practice-inspired-by-active-poses/#:~:text=deeply%20h
eld%20places.%E2%80%9D-,%E2%80%9CA%20restorative
%20pose%20is%20any%20pose%20in%20which%20the%20
arrangement,breath%2C%E2%80%9D%20says%20Jonina%2
0Turzi

Sama vritti prânâyâma. (2023, February 21). The BioMedical
Institute of Yoga & Meditation. https://biyome.com.au/pranaya
ma-manual/sama-vritti-pranayama/#:~:text=Sama%20vritti
%2C%20or%20%E2%80%9Cbox%20breathing,has%20many
%20clinically%20supported%20benefits

Mbbs, K. K. (2021, November 18). *Why do Navy SEALs use box breathing? 4 benefits, 4 steps.* MedicineNet. https://www.medicinenet.com/why_do_navy_seals_use_box_breathing/article.htm

Banyan Botanicals. (2023). *Nadi Shodhana Pranayama.* Retrieved December 3, 2023, from https://www.banyanbotanicals.com/info/ayurvedic-living/living-ayurveda/yoga/nadi-shodhana-pranayama/

Bisht, H. (2023, August 17). *Benefits of Ujjayi Pranayama (Ocean Breath) and How to Do it By Dr. Himani Bisht.* PharmEasy Blog. https://pharmeasy.in/blog/health-fitness-benefits-of-ujjayi-pranayama-and-how-to-do-it/#:~:text=Ujjayi%20pranayama%20is%20one%20of,sound%20like%20a%20faint%20snore

Meditation and mindfulness: What you need to know. (n.d.). NCCIH. https://www.nccih.nih.gov/health/meditation-and-mindfulness-what-you-need-to-know#:~:text=Meditation%20has%20a%20history%20that,and%20enhance%20overall%20well%2Dbeing

Stages of meditation. (n.d.). Do Meditation. https://www.do-meditation.com/stages-of-meditation.html#:~:text=There%20are%20nine%20stages%20of,back%20to%20an%20earlier%20stage

Conclusion

"In conclusion, the greatest investment you can make is in yourself. Keep learning, growing, and evolving."
-Unknown

I hope you enjoyed *Yoga for Relaxation* and now feel empowered to bring these techniques into your daily life. When you are at the office and a person interrupts your train of thought, you know an easy deep breathing technique to help you process anger or frustration as it arises. While lying in bed next to a snoring body, you will remember ocean breath and make hissing, Darth-Vader-like sounds to calm your mind.

As you move through your day, scrolling through news feeds, reading text and email messages, caring for those you love, you will pause if you feel overwhelmed, anxious, or unhappy and remember alternating nostril breathing. You will place your right thumb over your right nostril and breathe in and out the left side of your nose for 60 seconds to bring your awareness back into the present moment.

You now know from experience that slow, deliberate breathing taps into the relaxation response in your body, your inherent healing system.

In addition to learning about the history of yoga and the ancient Sanskrit language, you have also learned gentle yoga poses to help you sit comfortably, stand tall, and lie down in safe and healthy way. And you now know that meditation is as simple as turning your attention onto your breath.

Meditating as you walk into your home, while sitting in a chair noticing your surroundings, and connecting with your senses while lying in bed listening to a guided meditation will all serve as methods to help you rekindle your innate power and wisdom.

Practicing these exercises and techniques has hopefully brought moments of sweetness into your day and given you a renewed sense of health and well-being.

If you enjoyed reading this book, please take a moment to share your feedback by writing a review.

About the Author

Osha loves creating community and togetherness through yoga, song and dance. An East Coast native, Osha spent time in San Diego, California before returning home to the North Shore to start her family. She enjoys the seasons back east, spending time in the ocean, and you will usually find her out and about singing and dancing with her daughter. Osha offers fun and creative relaxation based classes in-person, online and through The Superbloom Podcast.

Made in the USA
Columbia, SC
18 December 2023

28738860R00054